Peggy Crysler
of Upper Canada

Christopher Moore

Grolier Limited
TORONTO

Cover illustration: Sue Wilkinson

Cover Photo: Metropolitan Toronto Library (T-30795) Cornwall, Ontario, 1845. Cornwall was one of the larger towns in Upper Canada, close to where Peggy Crysler grew up.

Photo credits: Public Archives of Canada, pages 5 (C-5586), 9 (15291), 11 (C-96361), 15 (1619-2), 21 (C-44633), 24 (C-34334), 35 (C-73697); Mika Collection, page 7; Metropolitan Toronto Library, pages 12 (T16542), 13, 32 (T-14987), 42 (T-16481); Black Creek Pioneer Village, pages 16, 18; St. Lawrence Parks Commission, pages 19, 20, 23, 25, 29, 36, 39, 41.

Canadian Cataloguing in Publication Data

Moore, Christopher
   Peggy Crysler of Upper Canada

(Heritage series)
ISBN 0-7172-2288-8

1. Crysler, Peggy, 1799–1868—Juvenile literature.   2. United Empire loyalists—Ontario—Biography—Juvenile literature.   3. Ontario— Social life and customs—Juvenile literature.
I. Title.   II. Series: Heritage series (Toronto, Ont.).

FC3071.1.C78M66 1988   971.3'02'0924   C88-093431-X
F1058.C78M66 1988

123456789   DWF   7654321098

Printed and Bound in Canada.

Contents

Introduction

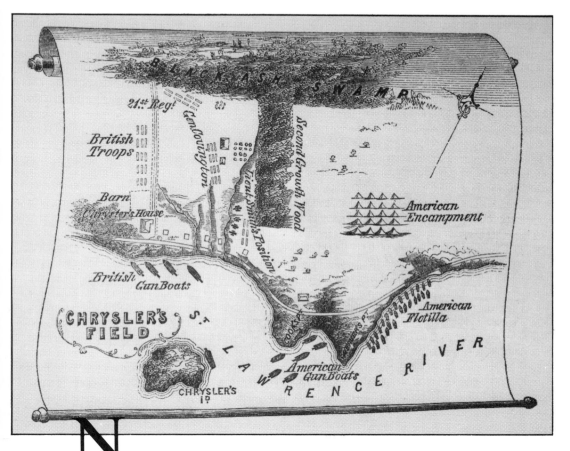

November 10, 1813. All day Peggy Crysler has been watching an American army sail down the river in front of her house, heading down to Montreal. Canada has been invaded. In the last few days, seven thousand American soldiers have gone by Williamsburgh in the sleet and the rain. All along the river, the Canadian militia, including Peggy's father, have been firing at the boats. No one can stop the Americans. But

This drawing from 1839 shows the approximate positions of British and American soldiers at Crysler's Farm on November 10, 1813. Note the spelling of Chrysler— each version is acceptable.

5

now something else forces them to stop just downriver. They have reached the wild rapids called the Long Sault, and they must plan a route through them. As they prepare, more boats full of soldiers come down the river and land on the Cryslers' shore. Peggy sees they are not Americans. They are British soldiers who are pursuing the invaders. Now they have caught up.

As the British soldiers land, their commander takes a look at the Cryslers' big stone farmhouse. He decides to make it his headquarters and orders his army to settle in for the night. Hundreds of redcoated soldiers put up tents or just lie down in the stubbly winter wheat in the Cryslers' fields. Peggy's stepmother takes Peggy and the other children down to the cellar for safety. There will be a battle in the Cryslers' fields tomorrow.

Suddenly the Cryslers' farm is a dangerous place to be. Bullets and cannonballs will fly once the battle starts. If the Americans come close, they are sure to aim at the buildings where Peggy and her family are hiding. The Americans might win the battle and conquer Upper Canada. The Cryslers don't want that to happen. They came to Upper Canada because of the Americans. They have fought them before. Wars with the Americans have a lot to do with who Peggy Crysler is and why she lives in Williamsburgh, Upper Canada.

Although she really did exist, Peggy Crysler was nobody famous. She lived her life the way a lot of ordinary people lived in Upper Canada in the early 1800s.

Chapter One

The Cryslers and the German Loyalists

Peggy Crysler's great-grandparents started the Cryslers on the path to Williamsburgh, Upper Canada. Johan and Katherina Greisler came to the British colony of New York in 1710, as refugees from a war in Germany, their homeland. Nobody in New York was able to spell or pronounce their name, so the Greislers became the Cryslers. All the Cryslers in North America—including Walter P. Chrysler, who built cars and started the Chrysler Corporation—are

No longer feeling safe or welcome in their American homes, many Loyalists fled north to Canada. They were people of all trades, from all social positions and grades of wealth who disapproved of American independence.

descended from Johan and Katherina Greisler.

The Cryslers and many other German refugee families settled in the Mohawk Valley. There on the western frontier of the colony of New York, they built farms and homes and raised families. The Mohawk Valley seemed a good, quiet home for the German settlers, and they lived there happily for sixty-five years. Then the American Revolution began. The lives of these settlers were destined to change.

All over the Thirteen Colonies rebels took up arms and colonists loyal to the King fought back. Britain sent more soldiers to the colonies, and they found themselves in a war. In 1776 the rebels declared that the Thirteen Colonies would become the independent United States of America.

The Revolution divided the settlers of the Mohawk Valley. Some joined in the rebellion. But most of the Cryslers were grateful to the King who had helped their families come to America. They knew they weren't oppressed there, and they looked up to the royal officials in the colony. Why should they be rebels?

In 1783 Britain had to recognize that the American rebels had won. King George III's Thirteen Colonies were now the independent United States of America. When the Revolution ended, the colony of New York became a state of the new nation, and there was no place in New York State for Loyalists. In 1784 the Cryslers, like thousands of Loyalist soldiers and their families, left their homes in New York for a new life in Canada. The Cryslers were refugees again.

Settling in Upper Canada

The Loyalists who fled to Canada settled in new communities in groups. Many decided to settle along the St. Lawrence River and beside Lake Ontario. By the end of 1784, six thousand Loyalists had settled into new homes in what would become Upper Canada.

The surveyors who went ahead measured off the land and divided it into chunks called townships. Every 16 kilometres (nine miles) along their map of the river, they started another township. At first they numbered them—1,2,3. Later each one was named for a son or daughter of King George III. King George had a lot of

Like Williamsburgh, most early communities in Upper Canada grew up along the shores of waterways. Water was the easiest means of travel.

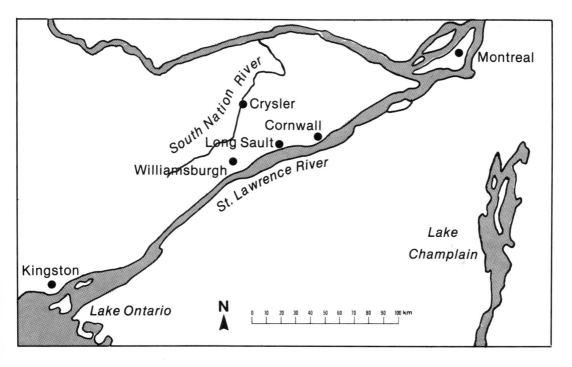

9

children. Soon there were townships of Charlottenburgh, Marysburgh, Adolphustown, Augusta, Matilda, and Williamsburgh. Many of the German Loyalists chose to settle together at Williamsburgh, facing the fast-flowing St. Lawrence River.

The British government wanted to help the Loyalists in their new homes. It had promised land to all the Loyalists who came to the Canadian colonies. One of the youngest of all the Upper Canadian Loyalists who received land in 1784 was Peggy Crysler's father, John. He was just fourteen, but he had been a soldier, and so he was entitled to land of his own. Along with his father and his brother Geronimus, John took his land at Williamsburgh on the St. Lawrence. He became part of a new German community and the owner of a forty-hectare piece of Williamsburgh Township.

The new settlements of 1784 grew into the colony of Upper Canada. In 1791, the British government passed the Constitution or Canada Act, which divided the old colony of Quebec into Lower Canada (where most of the colonists were French Canadians) and Upper Canada, where the Loyalists had settled. The next year John Graves Simcoe arrived to become Upper Canada's first Lieutenant-Governor. Governor Simcoe wanted Upper Canada to grow into a prosperous, powerful British colony. When they arrived in Upper Canada, Governor Simcoe and his wife were pleased to see how the Loyalist communities along the river were growing. As they passed Williamsburgh, Elizabeth

Simcoe wrote in her diary, "There are many Dutch and German families about here, whose houses and grounds have a neater and a better appearance than those of any other people." Those were Peggy Crysler's people.

Peggy's parents, John Crysler and Dorothea Adams, were married at Williamsburgh in 1791. Their first two children died as soon as they were born. Then they had three healthy girls, Elizabeth, Anna, and

Lotteries were held to determine which piece of land a settler would get. Fortunately the land along the St. Lawrence River and Lake Ontario was mostly good farmland so most settlers fared reasonably well.

11

Margaret, and a boy, John Pliny. Margaret, whom they called Peggy, was born on June 19, 1799. She and her brother and sisters were part of the first generation to grow up in Loyalist Upper Canada.

Elizabeth Simcoe, the Lieutenant-Governor's young wife, lived in Upper Canada from 1793 to 1796. She wrote a diary about her experiences in Upper Canada.

Chapter Two

A Child in Upper Canada

When Peggy was barely two years old her mother died and she soon had a stepmother. Her father had to remarry, for much of the responsibility of running a farm and a household was the woman's. A farm was a family business. John Crysler certainly could not do it alone, not with four young children around. In 1803 he married a local girl, Nancy Loucks, whose parents were also German Loyalists from the Mohawk Valley. Soon Peggy had a new brother, Samuel. Unfortunately, Nancy Loucks died in 1808, and Peggy's father had to marry for the third time. Nancy Finkle was the children's new stepmother. Fortunately, she lived a long time, and she and John Crysler had ten more children.

Most of Peggy's neighbours were farm families who were relatives or who had been friends of the

Durham boats were propelled by sail or by boatmen poling along the river bed. The rudder was used for steering.

13

Crysler family for generations. There were Crysler cousins nearby, and Peggy's grandfather Loucks had an inn just down the road. They all spoke German, and they would all have had a friendly word for Peggy and her brother and sisters.

Williamsburgh was a new community, but it was not a remote place in the wilderness. The St. Lawrence River, running past the Cryslers' door, was a busy highway. Durham boats—big, flat-bottomed barges that could carry tons of freight and lots of passengers—churned up and down the river. Going up toward Lake Ontario was a slow business. The boats had to fight against the current all the way. Often the passengers had to get out and walk, while strong oxen plodding along the riverbanks towed the boats through the rapids. One of the slowest places on the upriver journey was the Long Sault rapid near Williamsburgh. "The whole of the river foaming like white breakers and the banks covered with thick woods is a fine sight," said one traveller. After working their way past the rapids, the boatmen were happy to pause at the taverns of Williamsburgh!

The Cryslers' Farm

Like most of their neighbours, the Cryslers ran a farm. On most Upper Canadian farms, people grew wheat and corn, and raised pigs. They usually had a few other farm animals and kept a vegetable and herb garden and an orchard. A farm like that made work for nearly

Planting was done by hand at first but as agricultural implements improved and became more available the job was somewhat easier.

everybody all year round. Men, women and children worked together to handle the numerous chores of farm and household. There was very little leisure time.

In winter, when farm activity was less hectic, the men of most farm families were kept busy repairing farm implements, making furniture and most importantly cutting wood. It was cold, but woodcutting went much faster when the underbrush was bare. When the snow was deep, it was easy to haul logs out of the woods on sleighs. In fact, the snowy roads of winter were better than the potholed and flooded roads of summer. If the mill was far away, many farmers waited until winter to haul their wheat there for grinding. The women were not idle either. The winter was the time to catch up on cloth and clothes making and other tasks that were given less attention during the busy planting and harvesting seasons.

Women winnowed the wheat in the barn. In order to separate the grain from the chaff, the doors were left open and the mixture of grain and chaff was tossed in the air. The wind blew the lighter chaff away.

In the spring farm activity picked up again. Once the ice melted from the rivers, it was time to ship the flour and wood that had been prepared during the winter. As soon as the ground was dry, farmers began to till the fields and plant the new crops. In the early summer, everyone was cutting grass and drying it in the sun to feed as hay.

In the late summer, it was time to harvest the winter wheat that had been planted the previous fall. Also, many settlers worked hard to prepare newly cleared fields for planting.

In the fall came the main harvest, when all the summer's crops had to be cut and stored. Seeds for the next year's crops had to be saved and everything around the farm had to be prepared for winter. When the snow began to fall, men sharpened their axes and prepared to go woodcutting again.

Once the harvest began, women set about processing and preserving crops from the fields, orchard and garden. There were other chores too, and the farmer's wife took charge of most of them as well. The young Cryslers all helped their stepmother to manage. Peggy and her sisters and brothers tended the animals and the gardens. When Mrs. Crysler planned meals, she would send the children to bring meat from the icehouse, vegetables from the root cellar, and water from the well. Peggy would tend the fire in the stove. She would polish anything that could rust or tarnish. She helped to make and repair clothes and other household items such as candles, soap, quilts and sometimes butter. For such a large family there was always laundry to be done and cleaning and tidying as well.

In the fall, the children went to the swampy ground to pick cranberries—keeping an eye out for bears doing the same thing! They would pick apples, and help to peel them and set them out to dry, so that months later they could make apple pies. One of the Cryslers' neighbours was a man named McIntosh. In 1811 he discovered some apple trees in his woods that had very good apples. He tended the trees and started selling the apples—the first McIntosh apples.

Some tasks required the co-operation of more than just family members. Harvesting crops, building houses and barn raising were typical activities that demanded "bees." Neighbouring families would get together and organize a work party to carry out the necessary job. A

*Apple drying stands
like this one preserved
the apples for use
during the winter.*

group of people could get a lot accomplished in this way
and at day's end they could look forward to the host
family providing fine food and entertainment—a well-
earned chance to relax after the work was done. Since
leisure time was scarce, bees were an excellent
opportunity to socialize.

The Way the Cryslers Lived

A lot of what we know about the way people lived on
Upper Canadian farms comes from travellers who
wrote letters or books about what they saw there. Many
of the writers were wealthy people from England, and
often they were not very impressed with what they saw

on the farms in Upper Canada.

Some travellers in Upper Canada said that children there mostly went barefoot and wore homespun. "Homespun" meant clothes that were made from fabric that had been spun at home. Farm women would spin wool from their sheep to make woolen cloth for their families. They could make their own linen from a plant called flax. Many Upper Canadian farmers wore these coarse stiff linen shirts. The settlers could colour these homemade fabrics with dyes made from boiled leaves or roots.

Peggy Crysler probably wore some homemade clothes although her parents could buy clothes, shoes

Spinning wool to weave cloth took a lot of time but most families could not afford to buy much cloth from merchants or peddlers and had to depend on homespun.

and other items too, because many goods were available from the Durham boats on the river. On special occasions, Peggy probably wore some colourful calico, and maybe a bonnet and a few ribbons and bows. But most of the time Peggy probably wore plain, drab cotton and scratchy flannel.

According to some English travellers, Upper Canadian farmers were so poor that all they ate was the plain and simple food they grew themselves. Visitors were not very impressed with the fried salt pork, bland cornmeal, coarse bread, and thick tea that seemed to be what everyone ate, three meals a day. The Cryslers ate better than that. They had milk, meat and eggs from their cows and chickens. They could make their own butter and cheese or buy these things from neighbours.

Food preparation took knowledge, skill, time and patience. Peggy and her sisters would have spent long hours helping and learning to prepare food and plan meals.

They could buy preserved foods from the merchants and peddlers. Still they were used to a simple diet and were easily satisfied with the foods they had from the farm.

Early homes of settlers in Upper Canada were not very pretty or comfortable. A new settler usually lived in a "shanty," a simple, open shelter with just enough cover to keep the rain off. Once the farmer built a proper log cabin, the shanty often became a pigsty, but some families lived in shanties for years. Even a log cabin was small and drafty and dirty. Some had dirt floors, and they usually had only a couple of rooms.

A farm with a log cabin and fields cleared for planting took years to build. In this picture the building behind the log cabin was probably the original shanty.

21

The windows were small and covered with shutters instead of glass. Inside there was only homemade wooden furniture, and everyone shared the same few plates and bowls. The farm fields full of stumps and weeds started just outside the door. To the visitors, the whole place often seemed dirty and cramped.

Many Upper Canadian children did grow up in homes like that, but Peggy Crysler did not. John Crysler may have had a shanty and a log cabin when he first arrived. But before Peggy was very old, maybe even before she was born, the Cryslers had built a solid, stone farmhouse. It had a deep cellar, two floors, and several rooms. There was glass in the windows, and the Cryslers may have bought furniture and kitchenware and decorations from Montreal or Kingston, or from travelling peddlers.

Why did the Cryslers live in a big solid house, with lots of rooms, decent food, a choice of clothes, and even a few luxuries? For one thing, Peggy's parents were successful settlers. If the Cryslers' farm had not been successful, Peggy would not have grown up in Williamsburgh. People moved around a lot in Upper Canada, particularly poor people. Peggy was lucky that her parents had been among the first settlers there, with lots of relatives close by to help. Their farm was doing well.

Once the farm was running, the family found more things to do. Many travellers passed by on the way up to Kingston or down to Montreal. So the Cryslers started a tavern and a shop. In the tavern, they served

John Pliny Crysler, Peggy's brother, owned a general store which can be seen today at Upper Canada Village, in Morrisburg, Ontario.

hardworking sailors, boatmen and weary travellers. In the shop, they sold whatever they thought their neighbours might buy. Customers came in for a paper of pins, a plug of tobacco, a package of green tea, some allspice or a few peppermints. Women came in to examine rolls of cotton, flannel or bright ribbon. Country merchants sold everything from rum to eyeglasses. They often handled mail for their neighbours, so the Cryslers' shop became an official post office as well.

Wheat had to be ground into flour, and the Cryslers built a gristmill and a sawmill, too. Peggy's father began cutting timber, and soon he was buying forest land in the swampy country back from the riverfront. People started noticing that John Crysler

23

John Crysler often travelled to York and probably took his family with him. Visitors were impressed by the rapidly growing town.

was doing well, and they started giving him other responsibilities. He became a Justice of the Peace—what people called a ''J.P.'' J.P.'s helped to govern the townships and four times a year John Crysler and other J.P.'s travelled around the riverfront communities, judging court cases. Peggy's father was becoming a leader in his community. Soon he also became an officer of the local militia company. In 1804, the people of Williamsburgh and the four other townships that made up Dundas County elected John Crysler to go to York as their member of the Legislature of Upper Canada.

Chapter Three

Going to School, Going to Church

Several hundred people called Williamsburgh home when Peggy Crysler was a young girl. New settlers had cleared several rows of farms behind the riverfront lots, all the way back to the swampy ground where farming became almost impossible. Along the main road by the river stood the church and a few shops and taverns, but because most people were farmers, there was not really a village. There were no lawyers, doctors, or bankers to fill a village. When Peggy's father and the other J.P.'s held court cases, they usually met in Mr. Loucks's tavern, the biggest building in town.

Schoolmasters often set up a room in their homes to be used as a classroom. Furnishings were simple and basic school supplies were scarce.

There was no schoolhouse either. Most communities in Upper Canada were too small to have a real school. The people wanted their children to go to school, but Peggy was eight years old before the government of Upper Canada passed any laws about schools. Even then they only started four schools, and none of them was near Williamsburgh.

So what did people do? Very rich people could send their children away to Montreal, to New York, or even to England. A few sent their children to the boarding schools that had been started in the towns of Upper Canada. John Strachan, who later became the Anglican Bishop of Upper Canada, had started a boy's boarding school in Cornwall, just downriver from Williamsburgh.

Schools like John Strachan's could never teach all the children of Williamsburgh. Instead, small communities started their own schools. Someone would agree to teach the local children, and the parents would promise to pay what they could. By the time Peggy Crysler was getting toward school age, a German settler named Carl Koeller was going from house to house to teach the children of Williamsburgh. Soon other teachers opened small schools in the neighbourhood.

Peggy Crysler did go to school, because girls as well as boys went to little local schools. In some schools, the girls studied while the boys did chores. Then the boys went to school and the girls did their chores. In harvest season, everyone was too busy, so school just stopped until they had more time. Classes were quite simple. The schoolroom was usually in the teacher's home, and teachers had few books, blackboards, or teaching supplies. Students were supposed to bring their own slates to write on, but none would have used paper or pens very often.

Reading and writing were important in Upper Canadian classrooms. Most schoolteachers could teach their pupils to add, subtract, multiply and divide, and some went on to more complicated mathematics. Many teachers thought grammar was very important. Teachers who had travelled and owned a map or two liked to teach geography as well. Whatever the subject, most teachers believed that memorizing was very important. Peggy spent a lot of time reciting multiplication tables, competing in spelling bees, and listing the rules of grammar.

All the schoolteachers around Williamsburgh were men. Teaching, like most other paid jobs, was considered man's work. In small country schools, however, teachers' wives often helped their husbands, and within a few years, some women were running schools for girls in Upper Canada. Women taught different things to girls than men taught to boys. Mrs. Tyler, who started a school at Niagara in 1802, taught "all that is necessary for girls to appear decently and useful in the world, and all that concerns housekeeping." At Williamsburgh, teachers' wives probably taught sewing, needlework, embroidery, and housekeeping to Peggy and her sisters and friends. Her brothers, meanwhile, were improving their mathematics, or learning geography, or maybe even starting Latin.

Even if children only learned reading and writing in someone's farm kitchen, parents worried about what they read. The people of Williamsburgh, like many of the people in Upper Canada, had originally come from the British colonies that became the United States. When they needed teachers and textbooks, they naturally looked across the border. Yet Upper Canada was a British colony, and Loyalist families like the Cryslers had left the United States to remain under a British government. American books and ideas could be unacceptable. What if an American book praised the rebels in the American Revolution and called the Loyalists "traitors"? What if an American teacher praised the United States and criticized the government of the colony? Even in 1800 Canadians worried that there were too many American teachers and ideas in Canada.

Choosing a Church

In Williamsburgh the Cryslers helped start one of the first Lutheran congregations in Canada. At first the German settlers held their services in each other's homes or out of doors, reading from German Bibles and sharing the old hymns their ancestors had brought from Germany. Then, in 1791, Reverend Samuel Schwertfeger arrived in Williamsburgh from the United States. In gratitude, the congregation built a home and a church for the new minister.

St. George's was a handsome church. Most of the settlers still lived in log houses, but their church was a frame building. They had built it with boards cut in Williamsburgh's busy sawmills. There was glass in the arched windows that gave a view of the fast-flowing river. It was a church the settlers could be proud of.

After the church service, parishioners gathered to greet each other and exchange news.

Finally they had a proper setting for their hymns and prayers. Peggy's parents were married in the church soon after it was built, and most of their children were baptised there.

Pastor Schwertfeger preached in German, since that was the language most of his congregation spoke. At first his son-in-law, John Wiegandt, who became the next pastor of St. George's, did the same. But the new pastor worried about the children who did not speak German. English was becoming the language of the St. Lawrence River townships when Peggy Crysler was young. Young people learned English in school and in the community, and English was used in business and politics. Reverend Wiegandt started teaching the catechism in English, and he began to preach in English as well as German. These were just the first changes in the Cryslers' family church.

The Lutherans were just one of the religious groups that had taken root in Upper Canada. Some Scottish Highlanders and French-Canadians were Roman Catholics, but most of the settlers were Protestant Christians. There were Scottish settlers who supported the Presbyterian Church and Germans who were Calvinists. Baptist preachers and Methodist preachers roamed Upper Canada making converts. Mennonites from Pennsylvania settled at Niagara and in the Grand River valley.

Among these Protestant groups, one had a special position. Since Upper Canada was a British colony, most of its governing officials were British. Most of its wealthy and powerful colonists were also British. The Church of England or Anglican Church was not only their own church but also the official church of Upper Canada. Anglican schools, like John Strachan's, received special help from the government. Church of England ministers received salaries from England to help them build parishes in Upper Canada. The other church groups complained, but that was how it was. The Church of England was the church of the people who ran Upper Canada.

Once Pastor Wiegandt was preaching and teaching in English, he began to think about joining the Church of England. The Lutheran Church and the Anglican Church shared many of the same beliefs. As well, it was hard for a small community like Williamsburgh to support a pastor. Poor Pastor Wiegandt often did not get the pay he needed to support his family. The Church of England could afford to support its ministers and after careful consideration Pastor Wiegandt suggested to his congregation that they should all become part of the Church of England.

Some of the Lutherans in Williamsburgh did not want to join the Anglican Church where their German language and customs would disappear even faster. They wanted to keep doing things the way they always had. But most of the parishioners went along with their pastor. The Lutheran Church of Williamsburgh became part of the Church of England, and John Wiegandt became an Anglican minister. Peggy's family went along with the change.

Chapter Four

Upper Canada at War

The Battle of Queenston Heights was an important victory for Upper Canada but the price was high—General Isaac Brock was killed during the battle.

Peggy Crysler turned thirteen on June 19, 1812. One day earlier, the United States had declared war on Great Britain. The Americans were invading Upper Canada!

The causes of the war lay far away. Britain was at war with Napoleon, the Emperor of France. Since Napoleon had conquered most of Europe, Britain desperately needed to keep control of the seas. The British navy began to stop ships at sea, to make sure they were not carrying goods to Napoleon or hiding British deserters. American sailors did not like being treated that way. To get back at the British, the Americans decided to seize Upper Canada.

British troops, led by General Isaac Brock, stood ready to defend Upper Canada. But were the people in the colony willing to fight? After all, many were Americans who had recently immigrated to the colony. Many colonists often traded with the Americans or visited friends and family across the border. They were not necessarily interested in keeping Upper Canada British. The American generals planning the invasion thought they could simply walk in and claim Upper Canada.

It was not that easy. In Upper Canada, General Brock's soldiers were armed and ready. They went on the attack, and they won several victories. They captured American forts and rallied the native peoples to the cause. Suddenly it was clear that the colony would not simply fall into the enemy's hands, and that convinced many Upper Canadians to defend their country. At the end of 1812, Upper Canada remained unconquered, even though General Brock had been killed at the Battle of Queenston Heights in October.

Williamsburgh was on the front line of the war. By the summer of 1812, the Durham boats that travelled past Peggy's home were filled with soldiers and their equipment. The shipping on the river had to be guarded in case the Americans attacked. Peggy's father, a lieutenant in the militia, and the men under his command were kept busy protecting the river route. In September, while his men were guarding a convoy of barges heading for Kingston, the Americans crossed the river to attack it. Fortunately, the Canadians soon drove them back. Upper Canada wasn't going to be given up without a fight.

That winter, there were several attacks back and forth across the river. Williamsburgh was not directly involved, but it was not just fighting that affected the Cryslers and their neighbours. Because the armies needed food, farmers' crops were suddenly worth more than ever before. The war was actually good for farmers and traders, and some hardly cared to whom they sold their goods. Trade across the St. Lawrence River between Americans and Upper Canadians continued, even in wartime.

John Crysler, who had been promoted to captain in the militia, had to ensure that all his men turned out for militia duty. Not all of them wanted to, not when their precious crops needed tending. Often a quarter of the militia soldiers were missing. While he was busy with his wartime duties, the Crysler farm still had to be tended. Nancy Crysler and the children had to take over additional farm tasks.

In 1813, the Americans launched a new invasion, and Upper Canada's defences began to weaken. The Americans sailed into Toronto Bay and burned York, the capital of the colony. They sank the British fleet on Lake Erie, and they forced the British ships on Lake Ontario to hide in Kingston harbour. American armies drove the British out of southwestern Upper Canada and invaded the Niagara Peninsula. Then in the fall, they moved into eastern Upper Canada, heading for Montreal.

In September 1813, Peggy's eldest sister, Elizabeth, married Seneca Duell, a carpenter from another local

Loyalist family. Elizabeth was the first of the Crysler children to marry, but the guests must have talked about the war as much as the wedding. American soldiers were about to invade their part of Upper Canada. Would the whole colony be conquered before the new couple settled into their new home?

They soon found out. Six weeks after the wedding, at the end of October, the Americans came roaring down the St. Lawrence bound for Montreal. If they could capture Montreal, they could win the war. On November 10, Peggy Crysler saw the American soldiers going past in their boats. Then the pursuing British troops arrived at Williamsburgh, close behind their enemy. Suddenly the Cryslers' home became an army's headquarters. An important battle for Upper Canada would be fought in the Cryslers' fields.

Chapter Five

The Battle of Crysler's Farm

This mural, ''Climax at Crysler's Farm,'' was painted by Canadian artist Adam Sherriff-Scott in 1960-61. The mural shows the decisive moments of the battle as the British army charges and beats back the Americans.

Down in the cellar of the Cryslers' big stone house, Peggy Crysler did not see much of the Battle of Crysler's Farm. But neither did many of the soldiers who fought in it. Like most battles, the one at Crysler's farm was full of smoke and noise and confusion. Most ordinary soldiers hardly knew what was happening to them. Even when the battle was over, it took a while before everyone knew who had won and who had lost.

The British leader, Colonel Morrison, had only eight hundred men. The Americans had several thousand. But Colonel Morrison had one advantage. His men were trained professional soldiers, while the Americans were farmers and other workmen caught up in the war. On the wide, flat wheatfields of Crysler's

36

farm, the British soldiers could fight the kind of battle they were trained for. For once, the American frontiersmen would be caught in the open.

On the morning of November 11, the sleet and rain finally stopped and the Americans prepared to attack the army that had chased them. One of the first to see them coming was a cavalryman named John Loucks, a cousin of Peggy's first stepmother, Nancy Loucks. Early in the morning, John went on horseback to scout the enemy territory around Cook's Point. When he found the Americans marching toward him, he rode madly back to give the warning.

It was nearly noon before the American commanders sent their soldiers into the Cryslers' fields. The British were ready. In the cellar, Peggy and her family could soon tell the difference in the way the two armies fired their weapons. The American soldiers seemed to fire all the time, but the British regiments held their fire. When the enemy was close, an officer shouted a command and the soldiers all fired at once in a volley. The British fired volley after volley from their protected positions behind the fences. They made it impossible for the Americans to keep advancing. They stopped.

Then the British soldiers advanced. The Cryslers' fields had been ploughed and planted with winter wheat that would sprout in the spring. As the soldiers moved forward, the muddy ploughed ground sucked at their feet. Log fences blocked their path. All the time the Americans were firing at them, but the British soldiers continued to march forward. One group rushed ahead and captured the cannon that the Americans had brought onto the battlefield. That made it easier for all the British. The British kept advancing, firing volleys as they marched, until the Americans turned and ran. Only nightfall and the return of sleet and rain saved the defeated men. The British army had won the Battle of Crysler's Farm.

At once, Colonel Morrison had a job for Peggy's father, who had watched the whole battle. John Crysler was sent off to Montreal with news of the victory. His journey took five days, and by the time he returned, the Americans had abandoned their attack on Montreal. There would be no more American invaders around Williamsburgh.

After the Battle

After the Battle of Crysler's Farm, Peggy Crysler and her family may have felt victorious for a while. But a battlefield was a horrible place, even for the winners. In a few hours of fighting, hundreds of men had been killed in the Cryslers' wheat fields. Hundreds more had been wounded, and the Cryslers' house and barns were turned into hospitals for them. The soldiers who had survived needed food and firewood and shelter, and they helped themselves to the Cryslers' goods. By the time the army finally marched away, the Cryslers' handsome house was a ruin. Their crops had been trampled, and their grain and livestock had been eaten. Their barns and fences had been torn down and burned.

Many of the Cryslers' neighbours had suffered similar damage and losses. They had discovered what an invasion meant, and it made them angry. Some of them wanted to kill the wounded Americans. The Americans

This monument was erected to mark the British victory at the Battle of Crysler's Farm. It can be seen today at Upper Canada Village near Morrisburg, Ontario.

IN HONOUR OF
THE BRAVE MEN
WHO FOUGHT AND FELL
IN THE VICTORY OF
CRYSLER'S FARM
ON THE
11TH NOVEMBER 1813.
THIS MONUMENT WAS ERECTED
BY THE
CANADIAN PARLIAMENT.
1895

had come to Upper Canada expecting to be welcomed. Now, even as helpless prisoners, they had to be protected from the people they had come to conquer. As the American generals retreated to the United States, they were talking about the "universal hostility" of the people along the river. Although the War of 1812 dragged on for another year, it ended with all the American armies out of Upper Canada. The colony had been saved.

In 1814, John Crysler submitted a compensation claim to the government at York which included this list of damages and losses suffered in the Battle of Crysler's Farm. Happily for the Crysler family, they were generously compensated.

1.	Cedar Fences Burnt and Destroyed	£55
2.	Rail Fences Burnt and Destroyed	£35
3.	Hay and grain	£40
4.	Two Barns dismantled and sheds most of the boards taken off and burnt	£10
5.	50 Bushels Potatoes—20 (bushels) apples taken out of the hills	£10
6.	Swine, sheep and beehives	£15
7.	Two barrels vinegar for wounded	£5
8.	Kitchen furniture	£50
9.	House furniture and wearing apparel	£25
10.	Bed and Bedding lost and damaged	£20
11.	Use of 3 out houses, and stairs damaged and much ruined	£25
12.	Dwelling house as hospital damaged and very much ruined	£110
		——
		£400

Chapter Six

Peggy After the War

After the war ended, some of the Crysler children stayed around Williamsburgh. Peggy's brother John Pliny Crysler, the oldest son of the family, took over the family home. He married a local girl and they had twelve children, including three sets of twins. Like his father, John Pliny served in Upper Canada's Assembly. He also became godfather to a local boy, James Pliny Whitney, who grew up to be premier of Ontario. In the 1840s John Pliny Crysler replaced the stone house that had seen the battle in 1813 with a bigger brick building which he named Crysler Hall.

John Pliny Crysler built Crysler Hall, a most impressive brick home and a testament to his family's success.

41

Another of Peggy's brothers, Gordon, became a sailor. Their grandfather Henry Finkle helped launch the first steamship on Lake Ontario, and Gordon eventually became captain of one. By 1850, a canal had been built around the Long Sault rapids. Ships could sail the river between Montreal and Lake Ontario. Some of Peggy's sisters moved away from Williamsburgh. One married the editor of a newspaper in Cornwall. Another moved with her husband to Hamilton.

Peggy Crysler did not move that far from home. In 1818, when she was nineteen, she married William Loucks, who was a nephew of Peggy's first stepmother, Nancy Loucks. Peggy had known him all her life. They

The timber trade flourished in Upper Canada. Lumber mills cut the lumber into boards, planks, shingles and other useful products. Most lumber mills were water powered.

raised three children. A few years after they were married, Peggy and William Loucks moved to the wooded country north of Williamsburgh, where Peggy was able to help in her father's lumber mill business.

Canada was shipping more and more wood to Britain. Throughout the colony, woodcutters were felling trees and floating them down rivers to mills and seaports. On the South Nation River, the Cryslers and Loucks built mills to cut timber and grind flour. It was rough country. The roads were so bad that John Crysler said he was afraid to drive a team of horses over most of the bridges. Yet gradually a little community grew up around his mills. They named it the town of Crysler. By then John Crysler was a busy miller and the colonel of the local militia. Though he had given up politics, he was the grand old man of the county.

John Crysler stayed in his new town, but Peggy and William eventually returned to Williamsburgh. They were not very rich. They lived in an ordinary log house, not a stone one like Peggy's childhood home. Like most of their neighbours and most of their ancestors, Peggy and Williams Loucks were farmers.

Peggy and her husband lived long lives. The colony they had seen defended at Crysler's Farm grew and prospered. For years after the War of 1812, American immigrants were not welcome in Upper Canada, but newcomers continued to arrive. Some French Canadians came to work in the logging industry, and soon many of the people in the little logging town of Crysler spoke French. Most of the newcomers to Upper

Canada came from Britain and Ireland. In the 1820s, more than one hundred thousand English, Scots and Irish settlers arrived. They filled in the unoccupied farm lots and townships along the river and back into the woods. Roads and towns and farms continued to spread across what is present-day southern Ontario. The Loyalists of 1784 and their descendents became a tiny minority in the colony's population. During Peggy's life, the few thousand people of Upper Canada grew into more than a million.

After 1814, the Americans never invaded Upper Canada again, but there was more fighting in 1837 and 1838. A rebellion led by William Lyon Mackenzie broke out in the colony. Mackenzie believed that the complaints of the ordinary people would never be heard under the colonial system of government. However, many men who had defended Upper Canada in the War of 1812 gathered to defeat his rebellion. William Loucks was among the defenders of the government. In November 1838 he marched with Colonel John Crysler to the town of Prescott to help drive back a party of rebels who had landed there from across the river.

The defeat of the rebellion did not stop changes in the government of the colony. In 1841, Upper Canada became Canada West in the new United Canada. In 1867, near the end of Peggy's life, Canada West became the Province of Ontario in the new Dominion of Canada.

Peggy Crysler died in 1868. In her long life, she saw many more changes. Steamboats replaced Durham

Tending the vegetable garden was just one of the many chores that Peggy, like most Upper Canadian women, had to attend to.

boats, and railways replaced horses and wagons. Travellers rushing past didn't stop at the Williamsburgh taverns anymore. If they stopped at all, it was at Morrisburg, a new town that sprang up west of Williamsburg. Towns and factories were becoming as important to Canada West as country farms. Farm families did not have to rely on themselves quite so much, and their equipment was better.

Of all the changes Peggy Crysler saw during her life, some of the most important ones were those that took place when she was still a child. When Peggy was born, the Cryslers were immigrants and refugees in a colony that was barely more than a wilderness. They and their neighbours were struggling farmers, looking back to their old homes across the border. By the time she got married, Peggy knew she was an Upper Canadian and she felt at home where she was.

For Discussion and Activity

1. Interview some older people (parent, guardian, grandparent) to find out what kinds of chores they had to do to help out at home when they were children. Make a chart comparing these jobs and the ones you do now.

2. Imagine you are Peggy Crysler. Write a journal entry for November 11, 1813, describing what you hear during the battle and how you feel.

3. Work in a group to plan a barn raising or harvesting bee. Include work schedules as well as meal and entertainment plans.

4. Research to discover more about one of these important figures in Upper Canada:
   a) Bishop John Strachan
   b) Governor John Graves Simcoe
   c) Laura Secord

5. Construct a model of the Cryslers' farm as it may have looked on the day of the battle.

6. Refugees still come to Canada today to find a safe, peaceful home. Discuss with your classmates why Canada is a good place to live.

7. Imagine you are being transported back in time to Loyalist Upper Canada. You may take ten items with you to help the pioneer settlers. What will you choose and why?

Glossary

Bee A work party organized to carry out a task which required co-operation. Work was often followed by an evening of entertainment.

Catechism A book of questions and answers that gives a summary of basic religious principles.

Durham boat Flat-bottomed wooden boats used for transporting goods and passengers before the introduction of steamships.

Homespun Homemade, plain coarse cloth.

Immigrant A person who leaves one country to live permanently in another.

Justice of the Peace (J.P.) A colonist chosen to judge minor offenses, to perform marriages, to administer oaths and organize local government meetings.

Legislature Upper Canada's Lieutenant-Governor was helped to govern the colony by an appointed Council, and an elected Legislative Assembly, which represented the people of the colony.

Loyalist A person who remained loyal to the King and the British government during the American Revolution.

Militia An army of local citizens as opposed to professional soldiers.

Peddler A person selling goods from door-to-door, not from a shop.

Refugee A person who leaves one place and seeks safety in a new one.

Schooner A one or two-masted sailing ship. Schooners were fast and easy to handle, and many were used to carry cargo and passengers on the Great Lakes.

Shanty A roughly built cabin or shack.

Surveyor One who inspects land and lays out the boundaries of counties, townships and individual lots.

Volley During a battle, an organized shoot when all fire at once on command.

Index